Anger Journal

A healthy place to release
emotions which tie our mind
and heart up in knots!

By Tamara Kulish

ISBN-13: 978-1974227358

ISBN-10: 1974227359

Published 2017
Copyright © 2017 Tamara Kulish
Cover design © 2017 by Tamara Kulish
Original artwork © 2017 by Tamara Kulish

Sometimes we need a healthy place to release emotions which tie our mind and heart up in knots!

This pocket size journal goes with you so you can have it on hand for those tough moments when you might want to tear someone's head off, but REALLY want to handle your anger in a healthier way! — do I ?

There's plenty of pages to write, along with helpful prompts, and place to write out lessons learned from those moments. This is more than a notebook... it's a tool, not only to release those difficult emotions, but to actively work on finding solutions!

This journal can help you see patterns of thought and behavior, to help you find solutions! I recommend using the Joy Journal in conjunction with this journal to find balance in your life!

Date: _____

Anger Level: 👎 ⚡ 🌪 💣 ☠

What sparked my Anger? _____

_____

_____

_____

_____

_____

_____

_____

_____

_____

_____

_____

_____

_____

How did I react? (Continue on next page)

How did I react?

What do I need to do to help the situation?

What's stopping me from responding the way I want to?

Date: ....

Anger Level: 👎 ⚡ 🌪 💣 ☠

What sparked my Anger? ....

....

....

....

....

....

....

....

....

....

....

....

....

....

....

....

How did I react? (Continue on next page)

How did I react?

What do I need to do to help the situation?

What's stopping me from responding the way I want to?

Date:

Anger Level:

What sparked my Anger?

How did I react? (Continue on next page)

How did I react?

What do I need to do to help the situation?

What's stopping me from responding the way I want to?

Date:

Anger Level: 👎 ⚡ 🌪 💣 ☠

What sparked my Anger?

How did I react? (Continue on next page)

How did I react?

What do I need to do to help the situation?

What's stopping me from responding the way I want to?

Date:

Anger Level: 👎 ⚡ 🌪 💣 ☠

What sparked my Anger?

How did I react? (Continue on next page)

How did I react?

What do I need to do to help the situation?

What's stopping me from responding the way I want to?

Date:

Anger Level:

What sparked my Anger?

How did I react? (Continue on next page)

How did I react?

What do I need to do to help the situation?

What's stopping me from responding the way I want to?

Date: ....

Anger Level: 👎 〽 ☁ 💣 ☠

What sparked my Anger? ....

....

....

....

....

....

....

....

....

....

....

....

....

....

....

How did I react? (Continue on next page)

How did I react?

What do I need to do to help the situation?

What's stopping me from responding the way I want to?

Date: ....

Anger Level: 👎 ⚡ 🌩 💣 ☠

What sparked my Anger? ....

....

....

....

....

....

....

....

....

....

....

....

....

....

....

....

....

How did I react? (Continue on next page)

How did I react?

What do I need to do to help the situation?

What's stopping me from responding the way I want to?

Date:

Anger Level: 👎 ⚡ 🌪 💣 ☠

What sparked my Anger?

How did I react? (Continue on next page)

How did I react?

What do I need to do to help the situation?

What's stopping me from responding the way I want to?

Date: ....

Anger Level: 👎 ⚡ 🌩 💣 ☠

What sparked my Anger? ....

....

....

....

....

....

....

....

....

....

....

....

....

....

How did I react? (Continue on next page)

How did I react?

What do I need to do to help the situation?

What's stopping me from responding the way I want to?

Date: ....

Anger Level: 👎 ⚡ 🌪 💣 ☠

What sparked my Anger? ....

....

....

....

....

....

....

....

....

....

....

....

....

....

....

....

How did I react? (Continue on next page)

How did I react?

What do I need to do to help the situation?

What's stopping me from responding the way I want to?

Date:

Anger Level:

What sparked my Anger?

How did I react? (Continue on next page)

How did I react?

What do I need to do to help the situation?

What's stopping me from responding the way I want to?

Date:

Anger Level:

What sparked my Anger?

How did I react? (Continue on next page)

How did I react?

What do I need to do to help the situation?

What's stopping me from responding the way I want to?

Date:

Anger Level:

What sparked my Anger?

How did I react? (Continue on next page)

How did I react?

What do I need to do to help the situation?

What's stopping me from responding the way I want to?

Date: ....

Anger Level: 👎 ⚡ 🌩 💣 ☠

What sparked my Anger? ....

....

....

....

....

....

....

....

....

....

....

....

....

How did I react? (Continue on next page)

How did I react?

What do I need to do to help the situation?

What's stopping me from responding the way I want to?

Date: ....

Anger Level: 👎 ⚡ 🌩 💣 ☠

What sparked my Anger? ....

....

....

....

....

....

....

....

....

....

....

....

....

....

....

How did I react? (Continue on next page)

How did I react?

What do I need to do to help the situation?

What's stopping me from responding the way I want to?

Date: ....

Anger Level: 👎 ⚡ 🌩 💣 ☠

What sparked my Anger? ....

....

....

....

....

....

....

....

....

....

....

....

....

....

How did I react? (Continue on next page)

How did I react?

What do I need to do to help the situation?

What's stopping me from responding the way I want to?

Date: ....

Anger Level: 👎 ⚡ 🌩 💣 ☠

What sparked my Anger? ....

....

....

....

....

....

....

....

....

....

....

....

....

....

How did I react? (Continue on next page)

How did I react?

What do I need to do to help the situation?

What's stopping me from responding the way I want to?

Date:

Anger Level:

What sparked my Anger?

How did I react? (Continue on next page)

How did I react?

What do I need to do to help the situation?

What's stopping me from responding the way I want to?

Date:

Anger Level:

What sparked my Anger?

How did I react? (Continue on next page)

How did I react?

What do I need to do to help the situation?

What's stopping me from responding the way I want to?

Date:

Anger Level:

What sparked my Anger?

How did I react? (Continue on next page)

How did I react?

What do I need to do to help the situation?

What's stopping me from responding the way I want to?

Date:

Anger Level:

What sparked my Anger?

How did I react? (Continue on next page)

How did I react?

What do I need to do to help the situation?

What's stopping me from responding the way I want to?

Date: ....

Anger Level: 👎 ⚡ 🌩 💣 ☠

What sparked my Anger? ....

....

....

....

....

....

....

....

....

....

....

....

....

....

....

....

How did I react? (Continue on next page)

How did I react?

What do I need to do to help the situation?

What's stopping me from responding the way I want to?

Date:

Anger Level:

What sparked my Anger?

How did I react? (Continue on next page)

How did I react?

What do I need to do to help the situation?

What's stopping me from responding the way I want to?

Date:

Anger Level: 👎 ⚡ 🌩 💣 ☠

What sparked my Anger?

How did I react? (Continue on next page)

How did I react?

What do I need to do to help the situation?

What's stopping me from responding the way I want to?

Date: ....

Anger Level: 👎 ⚡ 🌪 💣 ☠

What sparked my Anger? ....

....

....

....

....

....

....

....

....

....

....

....

....

....

....

How did I react? (Continue on next page)

How did I react?

What do I need to do to help the situation?

What's stopping me from responding the way I want to?

Date: ....

Anger Level: 👎 〽️ 🌪️ 💣 ☠️

What sparked my Anger? ....

....

....

....

....

....

....

....

....

....

....

....

....

....

....

How did I react? (Continue on next page)

How did I react?

What do I need to do to help the situation?

What's stopping me from responding the way I want to?

Date: ....

Anger Level: 👎 ⚡ 🌪 💣 ☠

What sparked my Anger? ....

....

....

....

....

....

....

....

....

....

....

....

....

....

....

How did I react? (Continue on next page)

How did I react?

What do I need to do to help the situation?

What's stopping me from responding the way I want to?

Date: ....

Anger Level: 👎 ⚡ 🌩 💣 ☠

What sparked my Anger? ....

....

....

_____

....

_____

....

....

....

_____

....

....

....

....

....

How did I react? (Continue on next page)

How did I react?

What do I need to do to help the situation?

What's stopping me from responding the way I want to?

Date: ....

Anger Level: 👎 ⚡ 🌪 💣✳ ☠

What sparked my Anger? ....

....

....

_____

....

....

....

....

....

_____

....

....

....

....

....

How did I react? (Continue on next page)

How did I react?

What do I need to do to help the situation?

What's stopping me from responding the way I want to?

Date: ....

Anger Level: 👎 ⚡ 🌩 💣✳ ☠

What sparked my Anger? ....

....

....

_____

....

....

....

....

....

....

_____

....

....

....

....

....

....

How did I react? (Continue on next page)

How did I react?

What do I need to do to help the situation?

What's stopping me from responding the way I want to?

Date: ....

Anger Level: 👎 ⚡ 🌩 💣 ☠

What sparked my Anger? ....

....

....

....

....

....

....

....

....

....

....

....

....

....

How did I react? (Continue on next page)

How did I react?

_____

_____

_____

_____

_____

_____

_____

_____

What do I need to do to help the situation?

_____

_____

_____

What's stopping me from responding the way I want to?

_____

_____

_____

Date:

Anger Level:

What sparked my Anger?

How did I react? (Continue on next page)

How did I react?

What do I need to do to help the situation?

What's stopping me from responding the way I want to?

Date: ....

Anger Level: 👎 ⚡ 🌩 💣 ☠

What sparked my Anger? ....

....

....

....

....

....

....

....

....

....

....

....

....

How did I react? (Continue on next page)

How did I react?

What do I need to do to help the situation?

What's stopping me from responding the way I want to?

Date: ....

Anger Level: 👎 ⚡ 🌩 💣 ☠

What sparked my Anger? ....

....

....

_____

....

_____

....

_____

....

_____

....

_____

....

....

_____

....

....

....

....

....

How did I react? (Continue on next page)

How did I react?

What do I need to do to help the situation?

What's stopping me from responding the way I want to?

Date: ....

Anger Level: 👎 ⚡ 🌩 💣 ☠

What sparked my Anger? ....

....

....

....

....

....

....

....

....

....

....

....

....

....

....

How did I react? (Continue on next page)

How did I react?

What do I need to do to help the situation?

What's stopping me from responding the way I want to?

Date: ....

Anger Level: 👎 〽️ 🌪️ 💣 ☠️

What sparked my Anger? ....

....

....

....

....

....

....

....

....

....

....

....

....

....

....

How did I react? (Continue on next page)

How did I react?

_____

_____

_____

_____

_____

_____

_____

_____

What do I need to do to help the situation?

_____

_____

_____

What's stopping me from responding the way I want to?

_____

_____

_____

Date:

Anger Level:

What sparked my Anger?

How did I react? (Continue on next page)

How did I react?

What do I need to do to help the situation?

What's stopping me from responding the way I want to?

Date: ....

Anger Level: 👎 ⚡ 🌩 💣 ☠

What sparked my Anger? ....

....

....

....

....

....

....

....

....

....

....

....

....

....

....

How did I react? (Continue on next page)

How did I react?

What do I need to do to help the situation?

What's stopping me from responding the way I want to?

Date: ....

Anger Level: 👎 ⚡ 🌪 💣 ☠

What sparked my Anger? ....

....

....

....

....

....

....

....

....

....

....

....

....

....

How did I react? (Continue on next page)

How did I react?

_____

_____

_____

_____

_____

_____

_____

_____

What do I need to do to help the situation?

_____

_____

_____

What's stopping me from responding the way I want to?

_____

_____

_____

Date:

Anger Level: 👎 ⚡ 🌩 💣 ☠

What sparked my Anger?

How did I react? (Continue on next page)

How did I react?

What do I need to do to help the situation?

What's stopping me from responding the way I want to?

Date: ....

Anger Level: 👎 ⚡ 🌩 💣 ☠

What sparked my Anger? ....

....

....

....

....

....

....

....

....

....

....

....

....

....

How did I react? (Continue on next page)

How did I react?

What do I need to do to help the situation?

What's stopping me from responding the way I want to?

Date:

Anger Level:

What sparked my Anger?

How did I react? (Continue on next page)

How did I react?

What do I need to do to help the situation?

What's stopping me from responding the way I want to?

Date: ....

Anger Level: 👎 ⚡ 🌪 💣 ☠

What sparked my Anger? ....

....

....

_____

....

....

....

....

....

....

_____

....

....

....

....

....

How did I react? (Continue on next page)

How did I react?

What do I need to do to help the situation?

What's stopping me from responding the way I want to?

Date: ....

Anger Level: 👎 ⚡ 🌩 💣 ☠

What sparked my Anger? ....

....

....

_____

....

....

....

....

....

_____

....

....

....

....

How did I react? (Continue on next page)

How did I react?

What do I need to do to help the situation?

What's stopping me from responding the way I want to?

Date: ....

Anger Level: 👎 ⚡ 🌩 💣 ☠

What sparked my Anger? ....

....

....

....

....

....

....

....

....

....

....

....

....

....

....

How did I react? (Continue on next page)

How did I react?

What do I need to do to help the situation?

What's stopping me from responding the way I want to?

Date: ....

Anger Level: 👎 ⚡ 🌪 💣 ☠

What sparked my Anger? ....

....

....

_____

....

....

_____

....

....

....

_____

....

....

....

....

....

How did I react? (Continue on next page)

How did I react?

What do I need to do to help the situation?

What's stopping me from responding the way I want to?

Date:

Anger Level: 👎 ⚡ 🌪 💣 ☠

What sparked my Anger?

How did I react? (Continue on next page)

How did I react?

What do I need to do to help the situation?

What's stopping me from responding the way I want to?

Date:

Anger Level:

What sparked my Anger?

How did I react? (Continue on next page)

How did I react?

_____

_____

_____

_____

_____

_____

_____

_____

What do I need to do to help the situation?

_____

_____

_____

What's stopping me from responding the way I want to?

_____

_____

_____

Date:

Anger Level:

What sparked my Anger?

How did I react? (Continue on next page)

How did I react?

What do I need to do to help the situation?

What's stopping me from responding the way I want to?

Date: ....

Anger Level:

What sparked my Anger? ....

....

....

....

....

....

....

....

....

....

....

....

....

....

How did I react? (Continue on next page)

How did I react?

What do I need to do to help the situation?

What's stopping me from responding the way I want to?

Date:

Anger Level:

What sparked my Anger?

How did I react? (Continue on next page)

How did I react?

What do I need to do to help the situation?

What's stopping me from responding the way I want to?

Date: ....

Anger Level: 👎 ⚡ 🌩 💣 ☠

What sparked my Anger? ....

....

....

....

....

....

....

....

....

....

....

....

....

....

....

....

How did I react? (Continue on next page)

How did I react?

What do I need to do to help the situation?

What's stopping me from responding the way I want to?

Date: ....

Anger Level: 👎 ⚡ 🌩 💣 ☠

What sparked my Anger? ....

....

....

....

....

....

....

....

....

....

....

....

....

....

....

....

How did I react? (Continue on next page)

How did I react?

What do I need to do to help the situation?

What's stopping me from responding the way I want to?

Date:

Anger Level: 👎 ⚡ 💨 💣 ☠️

What sparked my Anger?

How did I react? (Continue on next page)

How did I react?

What do I need to do to help the situation?

What's stopping me from responding the way I want to?

Date: _____

Anger Level: 👎 ⚡ 🌩 💣 ☠

What sparked my Anger? ....

....

....

....

....

....

....

....

....

....

....

....

....

....

How did I react? (Continue on next page)

How did I react?

What do I need to do to help the situation?

What's stopping me from responding the way I want to?

Date: ....

Anger Level: 👎 ⚡ 🌩 💣 ☠

What sparked my Anger? ....

....

....

_____

....

....

....

_____

....

....

_____

....

....

....

....

How did I react? (Continue on next page)

How did I react?

What do I need to do to help the situation?

What's stopping me from responding the way I want to?

Date: ....

Anger Level: 👎 ⚡ 🌪 💣 ☠

What sparked my Anger? ....

....

....

_____

....

....

....

....

....

_____

....

....

_____

....

....

....

....

....

How did I react? (Continue on next page)

How did I react?

What do I need to do to help the situation?

What's stopping me from responding the way I want to?

Date: ....

Anger Level: 👎 ⚡ 🌩️ 💣 ☠️

What sparked my Anger? ....

....

....

....

....

....

....

....

....

....

....

....

....

....

....

How did I react? (Continue on next page)

How did I react?

What do I need to do to help the situation?

What's stopping me from responding the way I want to?

OVERVIEW

What seems to be the theme of the events which set off my anger?

_____

_____

_____

_____

_____

_____

_____

What are my triggers?

_____

_____

_____

_____

_____

_____

How can I change my life to reduce the situations where I feel triggered?

_____

_____

_____

_____

_____

_____

How am I doing at working on being more patient before I explode?

_____

_____

_____

_____

_____

_____

# of Days I experienced each **Anger Level**:

__ 👎 __ ⚡ __ 🌀 __ 💣 __ ☠️

Time to get a new book to fill up!

Check out other books by this author:

All books are available on Tamara's Amazon Author page at: https://www.amazon.com/Tamara-Kulish/e/B00IVWCAEI/

Thank you for buying
this book!

I hope you'll take the time to write a review...
Other readers need to read your review!